JUST REMEMBER ME

A COLLECTION OF POEMS BY

G. C. KANJILAL

Also by the author:

Who says you are there no more
The Picture of Innocence
Twelve Red Roses

First published in 2010

This book is copyright under the Berne Convention. All rights are reserved. Apart from any fair dealing for the purpose of private study, research, criticism or review, as permitted under the Copyright Act, 1956, no part of this publication may be reproduced, stored in a retrieval system, or transmitted, in any form or by any means, electronic, electrical, chemical, mechanical, optical, photocopying, recording or otherwise, without the prior permission of the copyright owner. Enquiries should be sent to the publishers at the undermentioned address:

EMPIRE PUBLICATIONS
1 Newton Street, Manchester M1 1HW
© G. C. Kanjilal 2010

ISBN: 1 901 746 61 5 - 9781901746617

Cover design and layout: Ashley Shaw

Printed in Great Britain by:
Digital Book Print Ltd, Milton Keynes, UK.

Dedicated in memory of

our Resi (Theresia)

Preface

In my third book of poems, 'Twelve red roses'. I wrote a verse entitled, 'My last piece'. Due to overwhelming requests from my readers and friends, I have continued to write, hence this fourth book 'Just remember me'.

Since losing my dearest wife, Nana on 2nd of April 1989, I have found solace in writing, and this continues to be so.

I am pleased to state that the sadder elements in my poems have become less, though the pain of my loss is just as vivid, and this is plainly obvious in the piece 'April Fool'.

One of my poems has been reproduced in Resnews, and another has been published in the Sandbach Chronicle. For that I am very grateful to Mr. R.S. Jackson, and Mr J. Condiliffe respectively.

I would also like to thank my son Arun for his unfailing support and encouragement. I sincerely hope that this book receives its share of welcome.

Cranage, Cheshire
December 2009.

G.C.K.

Contents

Tomorrow	9
Mandy, the hairdresser	10
The stars in the sky	12
The Sunset on the Rhine	13
My wife's Alarm clock	14
A further view of the Dee estuary from Caldy	15
Loss of a friend	16
The empty fish-bowl	17
An unusual experience	18
A Surprise	19
Two worlds	20
That Stormy Night	21
Christmas Lights	22
Nature's wrath	23
The Red Berries on the Holly trees	24
New Year 2005	25
A child's face	26
I am what I am	27
My eighteenth birthday	28
Bombing of London	29
Anthing good around?	30
People's laughter	31
A complete stranger	32
Blue is my Colour	34
A dream	35
Those long forgotten words	36
Christmas Lights (2)	37
The last will	38
New Year 2006	39
New and Old	40
My wife's last wish	41
That lonely crocus	42
A reflection	43
The four seasons	44
The World Cup 2006	45
Our visit to Cologne 2006	47
Rain on a holiday	49
In a cafe	50
The last leaf	51
Meditation	52
I sing along	53
You came to hurt me	54
Go, just go	55
Two lonely people	56
A whisper is louder than a shout	57
What is morally wrong	58
A Winter's Gale (2)	59
Mistakes in my life	60
New Year 2007	61
A sunny day	62
Dispiriting yet sublime	63
Hymie's 90th Birthday	64
The Kittiwakes of Dunbar	65
Attachment	66
Three streakers	67
Charity	69
Lonely and alone	70
Your whisper	71
Your call	72

So in love	73	Our Resi	93
A distant display of lights	74	An unwelcome Prince	95
Full Moon and I	75	The little Robin	96
Full Moon's company	76	April Fool	97
No poverty, no wealth	77	The beautiful pheasant	98
A little fox-cub	78	That Magnolia tree	99
New Year 2008	79	The crimson coloured Rhododendron	100
Footprints on the Snow	80		
Farewell to Harry	81	The unveiling ceremony of R.S.M.'s Wall of Honour	101
The Tajmahal	82		
My love	83	A chatterbox	103
Puppies in the Kennel	84	My 70th Birthday	105
Unfair treatment	85	There is that of God	107
A left-behind item	86	Gentleness and Humility	108
An unexpected encounter	87	Our visit to Resi	109
Love is lovelier second time round	88	Back to Back	110
		Just remember me	111
After Forty years	89	God's Blessing	112
New Year 2009	91		
A phone call	92		

Tomorrow

Tomorrow, tomorrow, and tomorrow
One day soon it will no more come
Bringing with it a trail of utter sorrow
Or carrying news, which are so welcome

No more to ask what tomorrow will bring
Indifferent tidings, real good, or very bad
Living through today's joys of Spring
At tomorrow, no reason ever to be mad

When today's tomorrow becomes my today
With open arms, I do welcome it so
It doesn't matter what comes my way
I have looked forward to, I let it know

Waiting for tomorrow, is such a special thing
Everyday in our lives with eager anticipation
Wondering every today what tomorrow would bring
Something so look forward to with all animation

Yesterday's tomorrow will be my very last one day
I do not have to wait for tomorrow any more
For all the morrows in my life, I can sincerely say
Thanked God for giving me them, whatever was in store!

JUST REMEMBER ME

Mandy, the hairdresser

Every three months, I take my Barnie for his haircut
Mandy, his hairdresser welcomes us with, a big smile
From within a large Kennel complex, she operates from a hut
In her ever smiling face, there seems to be no guile

A pretty young woman, she gives Barnie a huge welcome
I see my pet is gleeful, from his rapid waggling tail
He certainly knows he's wanted, soon feels well at home
As I leave him in her care, know he'll be treated well

Mandy employs two other young girls, of course to help her out
They are also very pleasant, and so welcoming to my Barnie
That he'll be treated well, leaves me in no doubt
I then go looking round the town, without anything to worry

When the barrier is removed, Barnie enters the salon
Sees a number of dogs waiting, while others are having haircut
Joins the queue willingly, does not require any persuasion
Waits patiently for his turn, from a cage in the hut

In almost three hours, past usually the hour two
I return to the salon to collect my pet Barnie
He had his haircut, looks fresh, and handsome true
I can't wait to get back home, as fast as can be

There isn't a single time, when Mandy wouldn't complain
His hair was too matty, or his nails unacceptably long
Wonder if she wants to have his cuts more often
As to my explanations, they all seem to be invariably wrong

Not wasting time to quibble, I then settle her bill
Barnie had a nice haircut, he was also looked after well
If he had his way, know from his action, he will
Stay on longer with Mandy, see from his waggling tail

JUST REMEMBER ME

We then drive back home, waving Mandy good-bye
Thanking her for the care, and for his haircut
To see Barnie so happy, of relief, I breathe a sigh
At least it will be three months, before we re-visit the hut

Once again we will make the journey together in our car
Mandy will greet us both, with her effervescent smile
She will welcome my Barnie, and make him handsome than ever
I will listen to her complaints, she knows they are futile!

JUST REMEMBER ME

The stars in the sky

So many stars I see in the yonder sky
How wonderfully they shine, as I do pry

Some are so dim, others so very bright
How peacefully they sparkle throughout the night

The moon is not up yet, will no doubt appear soon
Meanwhile they give light, removing earth's gloom

The moon is up now, is it to keep a watch
O'er all the stars, or their combined light to match

He does not need to worry, they are not his rival
They accept his role, and welcome his arrival

So many nights when the moon is not up there
The stars go on throwing their lights everywhere

The cloudy and rainy nights, Oh how I so hate
When they fail to appear, and don't keep their date

I look forward to the nights with eager anticipation
When they appear again, and I gaze in utter admiration!

Germany,
23.8.04.

The Sunset on the Rhine

As I watched the Sunset on the Rhine on a Summer's day
In Düsseldorf, standing beside the 'Pegel-Uhr' tower
I beheld a wonderful spectacle of his glorious ray
Reflecting as a dazzling white band right across the river

The tide was in, the river was majestically flowing
Boats and barges of all sizes were sailing along in the middle
On my two sides, two bridges spanning the river were so imposing
So many vehicles were plying, and walking were ordinary people

On the river bank on my side, so many activities were going on
In restaurants and cafes, people were enjoying their 'essen'
On the wave-pattern footpath behind, so many kept pacing along
On the few seats I could see, all the spaces were taken

Suddenly it became bustling everywhere, was it 'cause of the Sun
In his departing moments, he shone brighter than before
Instilling a new vigour in life, as if the day had just begun
Soon he would be gone, but his glow will remain kindled evermore

I was so enthralled by the setting Sun, emotions can hardly describe
Wondered how many others took note of his reflection on the water
Was the Sun at his best, as the dusk began stealthily to arrive
That dazzling white band across the river, how can I forget ever?

Germany,
28.8.04.

JUST REMEMBER ME

My wife's Alarm clock

Tic, tic, tic, my wife's Alarm clock ticks away
Standing on my bedside cupboard, the table-lamp beside
Working tirelessly non-stop, twenty-four hours a day
Not just keeps good time, but takes care from my side

I remember buying the clock, it was a very special occasion
For my dear wife, who was genuinely so pleased
On her bedside locker, it wasn't just a piece of decoration
Ticking away non-stop, it kept good time indeed

On my bedside locker, I too had an Alarm clock
Given to me long ago, by a very special friend
It also kept good time, with its non-stop tic tic
Alas, one day this had to come to an end

Time has passed, my dear wife is there no more
As my clock packed in, I was in need of another one
My wife's clock now, my bedside cupboard does adore
And ticks away ceaseless, as it has always done

Oh, how I wish my wife had not gone before
As my clock had done, rather I had departed first
Her clock outlived her, but mine is there no more
How we two now hold on to each other so steadfast!

A further view of the Dee estuary from Caldy

O mighty River, to see you in full flow
Standing with my friends, on your bank at Caldy
My heart leaps up, and my eyes do glow
To see your vast estuary full, O River Dee

On this bright Summer's day, as I look out
The current is so strong, with the tide in
On my left, I see so many fishing boats about
And on my right, gathered are so many boats sailing

Flowing so proud, on this bright sunny day
With no care ahead, the world is your oyster
Nothing on this earth can stand in your way
Nobody to check your free flow, O mighty River

I see the powerful waves striking against the bank
Can hear so well the roar of your breakers
I know that you're engaged in a child's prank
You are busy testing its strength, O valiant River

With the tide in, you may feel very strong
Whatever you think, strength, you must not misuse
You have to remember, it will not stay long
Once the tide is out, you are hardly of any use

Meanwhile you carry on, O mighty River
Give me the pleasure of your so very strong flow
Let all the fishing go on, and the sailing prosper
Let us all be proud of the Summer's last show!

Loss of a friend

O dear Friend, to know that you are gone
I am bereft, and so very forlorn

You may not approve that I do grieve
How can it be else, please do forgive

I'll miss our meetings, your unmistakable voice
Your hearty laughter as we did rejoice

So much to talk about when we would meet
Share our joys and sorrows, it was discreet

The news of your death, it was so sudden
For once I was shocked, and so very shaken

All our meetings, I will always remember
With fondness and joy, will cherish them forever

O my dear Friend, I will not say good-bye
Know will meet again one day, both you and I.

The empty fish-bowl

The empty fish-bowl, standing on the window-sill
Each time I look at, so very lonely I feel

The lively goldfish was swimming only yesterday
With hardly any care, how proudly he did play

With his waving little fins, and mouth frequently open
Bobbing up and down, so happy in his little heaven

In the mornings and evenings, his movement was very frantic
Obviously he wanted his food, it was not all antic

When I would sprinkle his feed, so very quiet he became
Could see him busy gulping, his movement so very tame

I felt I could talk to him, and he did reciprocate
We became fond of each other, he soon became my mate

The way he had to die, I cannot still believe
Jumping out of his bowl into the sink, myself, I can't forgive

Don't know how long he was lying there, I tried to resuscitate
All my efforts were to no avail, it was far too late

Each time I look at the empty bowl, my heart stands still
Wonder from his resting place, if the goldfish knows how I feel!

JUST REMEMBER ME

An unusual experience

We were on this train, travelling from Crewe to Birmingham
It was an August morning, weather was nice and warm

On our journey, the train did stop at Stafford
A few passengers disembarked, and so many came on board

Our compartment was full but for one empty seat
A young man who had just boarded, rushed along to grab it

He turned out to be a chatty fellow, pleasant and so polite
Until our journey ended, he gave us hardly a respite

He kept talking about all sorts, relevant and irrelevant
Even offered to buy us some snacks, appearing somewhat extravagant

A couple of stops were left prior to reaching our destination
When he spilt the beans, had just come out of incarceration

He was an inmate for a while in the prison at Stafford
Now I could understand, the reason for him going overboard

Why was he so talkative, at last he was in a world free
Why was he so generous, not just to my son and me

The train arrived at last, at its destination in Birmingham
We both bade him farewell, shaking his hands very firm.

A Surprise

Sitting on a chair, in our drawing room
Kept looking at the sky, I don't know why
All I saw was grey, a sign of doom and gloom
Yet I kept on gazing at the dull sky

Will it bring rain, or a shower of heavy snow
We were now almost in the middle of November
If given the choice, which one to select I know
It is the snowfall, most certainly I'd favour

I like the first snowfall, so crisp and white
It will wipe away all the earth's gloom
As I cast my eyes, everything will be bright
Oh, how I'd savour that sitting in our room

The rain I don't fancy, with its pitter patter
As I look out, it will be all gloom
Everything will be soaked, if there's a heavy shower
It would be all misery, everywhere will be doom

As I kept watching, suddenly the sky became clear
All the grey soon gone, it was all light
No sign of rain's gloom, snow didn't come either
Surprisingly out the sun came, and made it all bright.

Two worlds

It was a sombre mood as we left the city of Manchester
That being the eleventh day of the eleventh month of the year

Almost without exception, people were wearing a red poppy
When we reached Cologne, the spirit was distinctly happy

They were celebrating the first day of their Carnival
As we walked along, there was a discernible air of festival

In singles, pairs, and groups, people were singing and dancing
So many passers-by joined in the merry-making

Dressed in colourful costumes, the participants were having fun
That we were in another world, doubt there was none

My mind took me back to the distant days of the war
How two worlds could be so different, so near yet so far!

Written, sitting in the bookshop,
'Mayersche' in Cologne,
Germany, 12.11.04.

That Stormy Night

Do you remember that wild stormy night
The two of us lying huddled in our bed
With your arms round, as you held me tight
I felt assured, and completely unafraid

The winds were howling as never before
Thunder and lightning were truly rampant
But with your encircling arms, I lay secure
Totally unperturbed by their rave and rant

Did not have to ask you, knew for certain
Whenever I needed, you would be there
Never for a moment thought, something else could happen
That stormy night, so ruefully made me aware

You are no more, why do I think of that night
Why do I reminisce over and over again
Your protective arms, how they held me tight
In this stormy world now, nobody to ease my pain.

Christmas Lights

Christmas lights switched on round the beautiful big tree
Alongside almost a thousand stars adding to their decoration
In the vicinity of the Chapel of the Crewe crematorium and cemetery
What a wonderful display, such a source of inspiration

I will always remember that cold early December evening
When the lights were switched on in front of a big crowd
The atmosphere was sombre, yet festivity was discerning
Rain stayed away, in the sky there was not one cloud

People of all ages had gathered round the big beautiful tree
It was so nice to see the children glittering the occasion
Bereavement had brought us together, to exchange our thoughts free
And to welcome the coming of Christmas with all animation

As the living celebrated, what about the surrounding dead
I could see them become live, and gracefully join the rest
The lights had brought us hope and peace, of cares instead
What a wonderful get together, to wish the world the best?

Nature's wrath

It could be so devastating, the wrath of the Nature
On the 26th December 2004, we got its full measure

As we watched on T.V., the pictures of Tsunami
Defied all comprehension, what we happened to see

Nothing that came in its path, stood a remote chance
It was so awesome, the Nature's destructive stance

It was certainly hell-bent to cause a devastation
On a scale, beyond all imagination and description

That it easily achieved its goal, there wasn't any doubt
What was the purpose, can anyone figure it out

It made us question our faith, can anybody blame
We'll remember with awe and abhorence, Tsunami, the name

It was a disaster, unquestionably the worst of its kind
When it comes to Nature's wrath, so feeble is mankind!

JUST REMEMBER ME

The Red Berries on the Holly trees

The red berries on the Holly trees, in our front garden
As the Sun shines, how picturesque they appear
Could there be anything better, the harsh Winter to brighten
I look intently around, it is so bleak everywhere

I keep looking at the berries on the evergreen trees
In their thousands they are, bright red crimson
Far outstripping in numbers, the green prickly leaves
They glisten in the Sun, on this cold Winter morn

I remember the berries, when they were all green
It seems to me now, so very long ago
They are all crimson red, brightening up the scene
And to all the onlookers, putting on a wonderful show

We are now in the beginning of a cold hard Winter
Yet to come are snow, blizzard and unwelcome rain
I hope and pray, the crimson red berries will be there
On the Holly trees as ever, the season's gloom to lighten.

New Year 2005

The New Year has just come
We are now in 2005
Let us give it a big welcome
Let us all be gay and live

Whether in the lane or on the street
Let us wish a happy New Year
To all those we happen to meet
Hope they all have a lot to cheer

On my morning's walk, I go with Barnie
Say happy New Year to all the trees
And to everybody else we see
The animals, birds, and of course the bees

I know they all do reciprocate
As we wish them a happy Year
Tell us how much they really appreciate
That the New day with them we share

When we return home from our walk
My son readily joins us two
Barnie wags his tail, and heartily barks
Altogether we give the Year a welcome true.

JUST REMEMBER ME

A child's face

Each time I ask my friend about his Model-soldiers
His face lights up as that of a little boy
With the ardour of a child, he could speak for hours
Age has not dimmed his passion, neither joy

He remembers vividly the very first soldier he had acquired
How he and his little friend, would pretend they're real soldiers
Nothing else mattered, they would play undeterred
Time was of no import, it could go on for hours

Little did he realise, he would amass succh a collection
Over the years was given a few, and he bought the rest
An erudite Judge, now has in his proud possession
A collection of Model-soldiers, undoubtedly one of the best

I well remember the first time, when I saw his collection
Displayed so elegantly on shelves, in his spacious bedroom
He gave a detail commentary, with so much passion
His enthusiasm was oozing, removing all the battles' gloom

When we meet up with, now both in our advancing age
His passion for the Model-soldiers remains undiminished as ever
As my friend talks about them, in amazement I gaze
The innocent glow of a child's face fills me with wonder!

I am what I am

I am what I am
Please God let it so be
I don't honestly have a qualm
If others happen to disagree

When I speak to the others
I tell them to 'Be yourself'
What good pretending to be a winner
When you need all the help

If you happen to be weak
Do not pretend to be strong
Your world mav not be all that bleak
Try steadfastly to move along

May be you are unusually shy
What good is trying to be outgoing
Do your best, hard you may try
Don't let that be your undoing

Be yourself, refrain from copying others
Don't live in a world of pretence
What good is trying to make it alter
Do learn the meaning of forbearance

I would rather be what I am
Hope the world accepts me as such
Frankly I don't give a damn
Do not care for pretence as much.

JUST REMEMBER ME

My eighteenth birthday

Today is the year's fourteenth day of May
On this very auspicious day, I was born
The sun is shining, I will make the hay
Oh, how I greet the sweet sunny morn

At last I have reached the golden age 'eighteen'
I know is waiting the key to my life's door
All the bygone years, they are truly 'have been'
I've now grown up, am dependent no more

No more to hear, 'Do this, do that'
I don't have to listen to any tripe
The 'orders' are definitely a thing of the past
I am now at the ' steering' of my life

Now I can do whatever I like
I am now very much an independent person
I can tell the others, to go on their bike
If they don't agree to my conduct and action

I have of course reached the age of 'consent'
Can drive a car, the brand I do relish
Can visit a pub without any dissent
Cast my vote to elect as I so wish

With so much to do, and such freedom
So many may wonder, how will I behave
'With right goes responsibility', are the words of wisdom
Have learnt from my parents, will carry them to my grave!

Bombing of London

Switched the television on, it was a beautiful morning
The date was 7th of July, 2005, I remember it well
Could not believe my eyes, as to what I was watching
London was burning, it was a living hell

I remembered the locations, been there many times before
Tavistock Sq, King's Cross, Aldgate, and Edgware Rd. tube station
A bus roof ripped off, underground trains in flames, and so much more
It was so awesome, the scale of devastation

Never seen such a traffic-jam, people were screaming and fleeing
Any direction one looked, it was chaos and consternation
A catastrophy had befallen, London was blazing
What we saw everywhere, was beyond imagination and description

It took days to clear up the mess, 56 people were presumed dead
And so many were maimed, 'cause of a heinous act of suicide bombers
The fire and ambulance men, police alongside worked non-stop unafraid
On the 14th of July, people paid respect standing in silence, all the Country over

Recriminations made, blames were rampant, have we seen the end
Will the world ever be in peace, I have serious doubt
Justification of the bombing, however stretched, can anyone extend
Why did so many innocents suffer and die, going their daily work about?

Anything good around?

Do you like what you watch?
I am afraid, I do not
It's all talk, no action to match
How can I like, I see what

Do you like what you hear?
I don't know what to say
It's all gibberish, nothing clear
All I hear both night and day

Do you like what you touch?
There's no touchstone, I am sure
It's all cold, no feeling to match
I don't know why it's obscure

Do you like what you taste?
My 'buds are active, I know well
Why not genial, why do I hate?
How I wish that I could tell

Do you like what you smell?
I wish I could say that I do
For watch, hear, touch, taste as well
Wouldn't it be nice for smell is too

Do you like anything around?
Soon you'd ask me that, I thought
I know that good things are abound
Somehow they skip me, that's my lot.

People's laughter

To hear people's laughter in shops, restaurants, and cafes
Or as we walk along happily Cologne's Hohe Strasse

It is a wonderful feeling, there isn't any doubt
Oh, what wouldn't I give for a nice walk about

On a summer's day, in Cologne's bright city
Leaving behind our sorrows, where everything looks pretty

In the city's parks, 'peace' is the word
The flowers are in bloom, singing are the birds

We walk along leisurely the bank of the Rhine
The river flowing so majestic in glorious sunshine

In the Kölner Dom, so many candles we light
People walking about serenely, what a venerable sight

Oh, how I like to see the buskers of Cologne
What a joy they give to people, and we aren't alone

But most of all I like to hear the people's laughter
It does not matter when, or where it doesn't either.

Germany,
29.8.05.

JUST REMEMBER ME

A complete stranger

We were having our 'cappuccino' as usual in Cafe Sagui
It was a beautiful summer's morning in sunny Cologne
The other customers were having their treats as were we
Sitting round in singles, couples, and groups, we weren't alone

Presently walked in an elderly man with his spotty dog
Carrying with him a black satchel similar to mine
Drew a chair and sat on it, placing on a table his bag
Don't know what caught my attention, wondered if he was fine

His look was distant, face drawn, a white haired elderly man
Wondered if he had lost his wife, as I had done years ago
Perhaps on holiday, putting on a face, trying the best he can
Life must go on, what good it do to let the world know

Could not refrain, kept observing, was I really prying
Felt ashamed, yet didn't stop, could not help myself
Was my concern completely innocent, a sense of fellow-feeling
That drew me to him, not called for, wished somehow I could help

The waitress came, he placed an order, the dog lay huddled on the floor
A drink was brought, he settled the bill, was truly pleased with the service
Seemed to enjoy his drink, expressing relish, was despondent no more
Wondered if my impression was wrong, and had done him a disservice

Was he an elderly man, who had come for a drink on a bright sunny day
After a long walk, perhaps little tired, on his mind was nothing sad
What made me think the way I did, was I wrong all the way
How I wished I could have spoken to him, and settled things weren't bad

JUST REMEMBER ME

He then got up, his dog on the lead beside, on they both slowly walked
He gave him a biscuit served with his drink, the waitress had earlier brought
I kept looking nevertheless with all intent, not uttering a word
Little did he know, a complete stranger, left me with what kind of thought!

Germany,
1.9.05.

Blue is my Colour

Whenever I look at the deep blue sky
Don't know why, it lifts my blues
The deep blue sea, as I do pry
Like a magic, shifts all my woes

The deep blue sky kissing the blue sea
Whenever I see, I am truly in heaven
Nothing else is more welcome to me
My blues and woes disappear for certain

To see the bluebells dancing in the spring
In singles, clusters, and masses spread everywhere
The blue butterfly, rapidly fluttering its wings
Can anything be sweeter to the eyes anywhere

The blue peacock, with his colourful wings spread
In the ground of a park, walking so majestic
In a measured pace, high holding his head
To a beholder, young or old, it weaves a magic

A love-letter written in deep blue ink
From a man of any age to his beloved
Of a more wonderful feeling, can anyone think
In the recipient's mind, blue is imprinted

All the 'blues' round me, lift my blues
Blue is the colour, I like best
I thank them all for ridding my woes
Long may they continue at His behest.

A dream

They say it is so nice to dream
It is truly good for one's mind
It does not matter what is its theme
Least of all whether it's kind or unkind

Most people of course dream at night
There are some no doubt who dream by day
Could either he wrong, or are they both right
Should one be asked nevertheless to dream away

After a bad dream, getting up from bed
How can one feel good, all said and done
You may still be recouping, fuzzy is your head
Can one have a clear mind, with day just begun

Following a good dream, one naturally feels happy
Hope you will learn, it would not long last
Brought down to earth, you soon become unhappy
From a millionaire to pauper, you're transformed so fast

One cannot fail to ask, if dream does any good
Whatever you hear them say, and so very kind
Better to live in a real world, as one should
And face its turmoil, leaving the dream behind.

Those long forgotten words

Sitting on my favourite white garden chair
One afternoon on a bright summer's day
Those long forgotten words suddenly happened to appear
Tried my best, but could not push them away

Those cruel words, 'I don't love you any more'
Sitting in the garden, the air was so tranquil
Uttered so long ago, as she closed the door
Why did they appear, why do they hurt me still

Said in anger they were, I knew it very well
Thought I had buried them, it was years ago
Out of the blue they came, to hurt me so real
Why did they have to come back to spoil my day so

She did make up, so fondly I remember
It was so wonderful, truly coming from her heart
That moment of my life, so very much I treasure
The warmth of her embrace will never depart

Yet why did those long forgotten words return to spoil
Such a pleasant day, everything so rosy in the garden
It was peaceful everywhere, why did they have to embroil
Those words said in anger, I thought were truly forgotten.

Christmas Lights (2)

Another year, round another tree, another set of Christmas lights
How they all welcome the coming of Christmas, standing side by side
With the decorated tree of last year, what a wonderful sight
Such a welcome source of inspiration, to all far and wide

Almost two thousand stars together, enhance their decoration
People of all ages, children included, gather to greet Christmas
Last year's tree is alone no more, with an illuminating companion
Together they make the festive season,   all the more joyous

Mince pies enjoyed, carols sung, speeches are duly made
Early December's chilly spell seems to hurt no more
Sombre atmosphere casting aside, both living and the dead
Join the celebration in a festive spirit, as never before

Christmas lights bring hope and peace to people everywhere
What a wonderful get-together for the advent of Christmas
Goodwill messages are warmly exchanged for the coming New Year
In our good and bad times, pray His blessing be upon us.

The last will

Two little boys, so pleasant and loving
Grew up together in their parents' sweet home
They were two brothers, couldn't be more charming
Wherever they went, were so very welcome

The difference in their ages, was only two
They turned out to be both very bright
The younger followed the older, like a brother true
Hardly they were seen out of one another's sight

They attended the same school, and college thereafter
One after the other, graduated with distinction
The older decided to follow an academic career
To the younger one, 'business' was the attraction

They went their separate ways, got married, had children
Life could not be for both any more kind
Their parents departed, duly thanking the heaven
Playing their part, and leaving two close-knit families behind

Everything was going nicely, till bad luck struck
The younger brother became unwell, his illness was terminal
Inspite of all efforts, there wasn't any way back
Devastation followed all round, when the end was final

Though they pursued different careers, had remained very close
The demise of their parents, brought them closer still
Much to everybody's wonder, one day he took an overdose
To be with his younger brother, no doubt, was his last will.

New Year 2006

New Year 2006, we give you a warm welcome
Myself, my son, and of course our Barnie
Please bring us peace and joy, true and wholesome
And let there be plenteous goodwill between humanity

As I take my Barnie on his morning's walk
Oh, how I like to hear the birds sing
The rabbits and squirrels are already busy at their work
The sun shining brightly, what a joy he brings

The trees on both sides of the lane, standing so bare
As we approach them, they say a big 'Hello'
We also wish them all a very happy New Year
Their cold faces soon warm up in glow

When we reach the cottage, meet Sylvia and Bramble
Barnie darts towards the later, to wish a happy New Year
With her toothache and cold, Sylvia seems to struggle
Having wished her a happy Year, I ask her to take care

At the end of our walk, when we return home
I see my son patiently waiting for us two
The three of us once again, give the Year a welcome
Please God be kind to us all the year through.

New and Old

Once again the New Year is upon us
The old year has just departed alas

Wonder what the New Year will bring
The old one hasn't been all joys of spring

Will there be more of peace and goodwill
Or will we see unrest and acrimony still

Will there be more of joy and laughter
Or will there be sadness and more of tears

Will we have more of success than failure
Will there be less of Nature's wrath to endure

The old year has seen almost everything
Still lives the hope there's always spring

Regardless of what it brings, we welcome the New
As to the old one, say a fond adieu!

JUST REMEMBER ME

My wife's last wish

So many things, I wanted to say
So much had remained unsaid
All through the night and day
As I lay unwell in my bed

In my heart, I perfectly knew
The time for me, was fast approaching
To leave this world for one new
Even though I had no yearning

You didn't make time to listen
I knew that you would regret
You might chasten yourself even
For me, it would be far too late

Could it be you didn't want to join
Did not think that I'd suffer in silence
Felt it might diminish my pain
Surely 'sharing' was an act of prudence

One day soon, you'd come to realize
Sharing our joys and sorrows together
As we had done, was truly wise
What good regretting, the past wouldn't alter?

That lonely crocus

That lonely crocus, standing on the green verge
Each time I look at, as I pass by
With a big smile, gives me an urge
To battle on with life, I don't know why

Colour light violet, standing on his own
From the passers-by, he does not need any pity
For his lonely status, he does not bemoan
Carries on with all vigour, performing his duty

Standing in the corner, tells me to pick up courage
Don't know how he knows that I am all alone
I like his beautiful face, he does assuage
Each time I look, my pain is all gone

As I pass by, can't fail to wonder
For how many other people, he is an example
Evan though on his own, he does not falter
From encouraging to carry on with their struggle

Soon he would be gone, that lonely beautiful crocus
Oh how I will miss him, I cannot refrain
From his isolate position, how so many of us
He urged to stand up to all our pains.

A reflection

Those youthful days, oh, how they come back
As I grow old with one foot in grave
The two of us were like Jill and Jack
You were such a sweet lass, and me so brave

How we used to attend the same old school
Hold our hands, as we walked together
You'd keep a straight face, as I acted a fool
Those wonderful days of youth, come back so clear

Your unrestrained laughter was for all to see
It would brighten up my world, in more ways than one
Hoped it was for, no one else but me
Would cherish evermore, till my days are done

That very first kiss, how can I forget
Lingers with me still, as if it was yesterday
I so fondly remember, it was our first date
Wondered if it was real, even to this day

Why all that ended, how I would like to know
Why do they come back, as my end draws near
We were Jack and Jill, in love truly so
As I reflect, why is in my eye a tear?

The four seasons

Oh, how I welcome the four seasons of the year
One after the other, as and when they appear

It is so nice to see the Winter's first snowfall
When everything is white, trees, rooftops and all

Even the Winter's gale, blizzard, and heavy rain
Somehow they soothe away all my pain

When the earth is new, as comes the Spring
With new vigour in hearts, new lives in full swing

It certainly for me is the year's best season
To say it is not, can one find a reason?

As I feel the warmth of the coming Summer
So many joyous faces, fill me with pleasure

How they enjoy, the beating down of the Sun
All through the day, having so much fun

When the Autumn comes, oh, how I hail
The display of colours, weaving a magic spell

Wherever one looks, it is gold and brown
The tree-leaves sparkle, the nature wearing a crown

Can anyone feel different with the four seasons?
However hard I try, cannot find a reason.

JUST REMEMBER ME

The World Cup 2006

The country was gripped with the World Cup fever
10th June-9th July, 'Here we come'
Germany, the host country was prepared as ever
Extended to 32 countries of the World heartiest welcome

Who will win the Cup, was on everyone's lips
Countries of Africa and Asia, would they get a look in
England were the hot favoutrites, so said the tips
With a contest between Europe and Sth. America, wonder who'd win

From the beginning simply England didn't live upto their reputation
An own goal by Paraguay spared their blushes indeed
Trinidad and Tobago held them for 80 minutes, Sweden couldn't be won
Beckham's 'wonder goal' against Ecuador, gave them the much needed lead

Having somehow seen off the Sth. Americans, Europe's turn was next
Portugal had to be beaten for England to reach the semi-final
The media-hype between Scolari and Eriksson was at its highest
The country waited with a bated breath for a victory after all

Ninety minutes didn't produce a goal, there were then extra thirty
Both sides played their guts out, but the position stayed as before
The match was next to be decided by a shoot-out of penalty
England sadly blew their chances, when three strikers couldn't score

The match was full of incidents, which did not help England
For his 'sins', their main striker was shown a red card
With Beckham limping off, no one was left to wave a magic wand
Three penalty shooters missing their chances made life real hard

England's dream of winning the 2006 World Cup sadly ended in tears
Recriminations were rife as expected both on and off the field
Eriksson couldn't take the country past quarter~final in five years
Beckham resigned from his Captaincy, it was time for a new team to build

JUST REMEMBER ME

Even though poor early performers, Italy won the World Cup
France were runners-up, in a game marred by a red card for their Captain
The host country Germany were third, they wouldn't easily give up
Portugal were the fourth, a position they fought hard to obtain

As for myself, over four weeks was glued to the Telly
Saw the World players at their best, at their worst too
The supporters were wonderful, the atmosphere couldn't be more lively
Have to wait another four years to see if England's dream comes true.

P.S.

Plentiful jokes were about, even though England were beaten
'Saddam Hussein has been found guilty, he was to face a firing-squad
Guess the three members of that, who have been meticulously chosen
You don't have to go far they are Lampard, Carragher and Gerrard'.

Our visit to Cologne 2006

When you re-visit a place, it is never the same
So many things found missing, saw so many new names

On our visit to Cologne in the summer of 2006
We were not just taken aback, were hit for a real six

The scale of changes we saw, our eyes, we couldn't believe
Wherever we went, hardly there was a reprieve

We arrived at Köln Hauptbahnof round about the midnight
So many new shops we saw, some old ones were not on sight

Walking out of the Bahnof, saw a huge big construction
Building of an underground line was relentlessly going on

There was even a face-lift when we reached our hotel
A new receptionist checked us in, didn't speak English well

Our room has a bathroom, fitted in brand new
One of the best in similar hotels, the owner prided when spoken to

Even the Kölner Dom, has seen big changes inside
Several sections have been created to house effigies with relics beside

Three things I missed most, on this visit to Cologne
Porcelain display in Kristall Passage, Auktions Haus, and Alt Köln

Kristall Passage and Auktions Haus, I used to visit almost daily
In Alt Köln, traditional German dishes served by waiters, so friendly

In between still saw many old things, and of course some old faces
The vast change hadn't caught them, retained their graces

JUST REMEMBER ME

I know change is a part of life, and we have no escape
Don't know why felt so sad, perhaps at the massive reshape

Perhaps as well to realize, nothing on this earth lasts for ever
One day it is so real and living, next gone forever!

On the whole we had a good holiday, and were glad to return home
One thing had not changed, Barnie gave us a hearty welcome.

Germany,
28.8.06.

Rain on a holiday

Rain, rain, rain, it rained almost everyday
Nevertheless it could not spoil our holiday

We visited our regular places, as we should
Tried very hard, not stop that rain could

The place I used to sit on the bank of the Rhine
Somehow was dry, was it a hand of divine

I would keep looking both near and far
Tried its best, but rain could not mar

Moored was Strolch with flags, on my side
There was Colonia 6, anchored beside

How often I have been on 'rundfahrten'
Didn't go this time, somehow it didn't sadden

The memories of yester year, came back alive
Rain could not dampen, hardest it did strive

I looked at the Messe-tower, so many cranes beside
Massive building work was going on, on the river's two sides

The trains on the Hohenzollern Brücke were running every minute
I could see them clear, rain could not hinder it

The Rhine flowed on majestically, as she has always done
Huge barges with heavy cargoes steadfastly rolled on

Presently near me came a pigeon, as if to say 'Hello'
'Don't worry about the rain', said as it paced slow

Sitting in my usual place, I saw the world pass by
Rain could not frustrate, hardest it did try!

Germany,
30.8.06.

JUST REMEMBER ME

In a cafe

So many people came, so many people went
So many sat tight, so many lavishly spent

So many people drank, so many people ate
So many just do nothing, simply sat in wait

So many were in a hurry, so many so slow
So many did worry, so many didn't show

So many were smart, so many dishevelled
So many did enjoy, so many bitterly complained

So many were old, so many were young
So many were right, so many could do no wrong

The waiters and waitresses served politely so many
They spoke gently, showed no dislike to any

That is how I saw life, sitting in a cafe
Wondered what would be like as ends the day!

Germany,
2.9.06 .

The last leaf

The last leaf of the tree would be soon gone
The tree would stand there bereft and forlorn

With the Autumn gone, the Winter truly here
As I look out, it is bleak everywhere

I ask myself, why the leaf has to go
The answer I get that it has to be so

The last leaf no doubt has outlived the rest
To cling to the tree firm, tried its very best

It certainly knew, one day its time would come
Will have to part, leaving the tree lonesome

Was that the reason, it found hard to go
Or the thought of dying, couldn't bear so

Wondered how the tree felt losing its last leaf
Did it sense likewise, was there a note of grief

When the Spring comes again, will have new leaves
Would its suffering end, as it hails the greens

Would it nevertheless reminisce, the loss of its last leaf
While welcoming the new, would it still be in grief

To the last leaf alas I say a fond farewell
There is a tear in my eye, as tolls the bell

One day no doubt, the tree's own turn would come
Won't face gains and losses, will be no more lonesome

Wonder if still living, what would I say
'There has to be inevitably an end to the day!'

Meditation

That beautiful white marble figurine of Meditation
Standing in a shelf-corner, in our drawing room
Is such a delightful source of inspiration
Wipes away at a stroke, all my mind's gloom

That graceful statuette gives me so much pleasure
I can look for hours, my eyes do not tire
What's she meditating about, oh how I wonder
Wish I could read her mind, and not despair

Is she in a deep thought about 'peace on earth'
Or is she praying for her own peace of mind
Why so much hate and destruction, why so little mirth
Beseeching God to give sense to all mankind

Is she so distressed, that can stand no more
Appealing to the Almighty to give strength to muster
That she can inspire the world as never before
To bring 'peace on earth', with people joining hands together

I think of the Artist, who made her possible
Was he thinking alike, how I would like to know
Was he appalled at the wanton events, so horrible
Was he as well asking for peace, how I wish so

Oh, how I pray that the statuette achieves her ambition
Standing in the shelf-corner, in our drawing room
To me certainly, she is a true source of inspiration
Each time I look, disappears all my mind's gloom!

I sing along

I sing along in my carefree way
May not sound nice, may be out of tune
It matters not, what others may say
Should they decide to listen, or run away soon

I sing along to my heart's content
Not to others, to give pleasure
So long I could give full vent
To my feelings, nothing else matters

I sing along, unconcerned and free
The notes may be completely out of place
Those who hear, may not at all agree
I am so at ease with my voice

As I sing along, I can't but wonder
What would happen if everyone was in tune.
It's just as well, I am the loner
For them to appreciate, the right note soon

Isn't it fair that there's both right and wrong
For us to understand the value of the right
I may be content the way I sing along
A wrong tune is not wanted, sing anyway I might.

JUST REMEMBER ME

You came to hurt me

You came to hurt me, instead got yourself hurt
Wasn't it deserving, and rightfully just

Wouldn't have been better to let things as they were
Rather than playing again, your customary overture

You decided to part, I didn't want you to
Why did you come back, what made you so do

Was it your conscience, realizing at last your mistake
Or was it greed, came back more to take

It was the latter, as it plainly turned out
Some people never learn, things how to go about

Hope you recognized at last, that nobody is indispensible
Moreso when one is wrong, arrogant, and unreasonable

You left me all alone, can't hurt me any more
Now it is my turn, everything between us is o'er!

Go, just go

Go, go, go, if you must go
I don't have anything to say
In your mind, you have decided so
I would not stand in your way

Our times together, what good to remind
Know they will fall on deaf ears
Just as well leave them behind
I'll save them rest of my years

I won't plead, neither beg you to stay
You have chosen, it is your wish
You have planned it all the way
Do just go, find another niche

I will not shed any tear
Will not try to hold you back
I will carry on, have no fear
Go, just go, wish you good luck!

Two lonely people

Two lonely people, oh how they meet
Two desolate hearts, on a Winter's day
Two pairs of sad eyes, oh how they greet
Two bereft souls, push their cares away

The first snowfall, I see in Winter
My heart leaps up, as I behold
Not a creature in sight, where have they gone I wonder
My longing arms, want someone to hold

Presently from nowhere, comes this pretty girl
Am I dreaming, or is it happening real
Walking alone she is, in this snowbound world
Suddenly she stumbles, I can hear her yell

I run along fast, extend her my hand
She does not reject, our eyes first meet
The predicament she is in, I do understand
I am grateful, that her she lets me lift

I feel as if have known her for years
We exchange our thoughts, surprisingly similar
Our lives happen to be, yet in our eyes no tears
Two lonely people, we walk along together.

A whisper is louder than a shout

A whisper is louder than a shout
Has one wondered the reason why
One day tried to figure it out
Did not have to look to the sky

For help; there was no need
The explanation was patently clear
Glaringly transparent, it was indeed
A shout can never beat a whisper

Tried to fathom how whisper works
A man meets his friend's wife
Completely innocent, about nothing to talk
Soon regardless, takes its toll on life

Whisper travels from one friend to another
In no time gets out of control
Reaches his own wife, sooner than later
No need there for work of a mole

The wife then confronts her husband
Naturally he denies all about it
The damage irretrievable, whose was the hand
Not shout's, whisper was the culprit!

What is morally wrong

What is morally wrong, cannot be politically right
Thus spoke years ago, the wise Politician, John Bright

Attacking, unprovoked, another country as Bush arrogantly done
Blair joining blindfolded disregarding unprecedented opposition

They gave explanation, which turned out to be futile
Possessing weapons of mass destruction, said Saddam Hussein was vile

A militarily ineffective country, they attacked with all might
The slogan was 'Shock and Awe', claimed they were politically right

Struck with horror and shock, the world declared them morally wrong
Who takes care of 'morality', when one is militarily strong?

A Winter's Gale (2)

The wind was howling, it was a Winter's gale
Went to look outside, encountered sheer hell

I had heard a loud 'bang', which made me go
The storm was fiercely raging, never seen before so

The trees were frenziedly swaying from side to side
One of the hedges was, completely broken standing beside

Felt any moment the house itself would come down
Fortunately bore the brunt, it was not blown

There were a few piles of old papers, on the garden seat
Thought were reasonably secure, covered by a thick plastic sheet

The latter was blown away, papers strewn all over
I decided to gather them, despite the atrocious weather

It took me a while before I picked them one by one
Made sure the grounds were tidy, left behind was none

Amongst the scattered papers, came across an envelope
The handwriting looked familiar, didn't know what to hope

Soon after came inside, in peace opened the letter
It was from an old friend, I had visited years earlier

She had expressed sincere thanks, upon my first visit
I was so moved, tears from eyes could not resist

Having passed away years ago, suddenly she came so close
Memories came flooding back, of them I could not dispose

Notwithstanding the ravages caused, I thanked the Winter's gale
For bringing us fleetingly together, after facing sheer hell.

Mistakes in my life

So many mistakes, I have made in my life
Resting in bed one Sunday morning
In their numbers, they were so rife
One after another, they kept on returning

Tried my best to push them away
They were far too many to dispense
Why was I in. bed resting anyway
Why they kept coming, what was the sense

I tried to reason, it was no good
Excuses and explanations were to no avail
I even thought of being brusque and rude
Yet I knew that they would prevail

The mistakes kept coming, they wouldn't relent
In desperation, I got out of bed
I had my share, yet did repent
Accepting they'll follow me till I am dead

I also recognized that they will come and go
Whatever I do, prevent that would not
They will be part of my life, how well I know
Regrets and laments, that's now I have got!

New Year 2007

We are now in the year 2007
Let us welcome it with an open heart
Let it bring for us, peace unbroken
And health, and prosperity, the whole year to last

Barnie and I go on our daily morning's walk
We say happy New Year to everybody we meet
The birds, the bees, the animals at work
And the trees in the woods, we happily greet

I know they freely do reciprocate
Say happy New Year to the two of us
The sun is up, he cannot wait
To wish us as well, as we leisurely pass

Down the lane, we see Barnie's friend, Bramble
He is in a hurry to say "Happy New Year'
Pulls his lead strong, and begins to scramble
We both run fast to say "Hello" to her

At the end of our walk, we return home
My son is waiting to say 'Happy New Year'
The three of us give the year a warm welcome
And ask for His blessing, as we say a prayer.

JUST REMEMBER ME

A sunny day

The night has ended, daylight is here
The birds are chirping, I hear everywhere

So happy and gay, they are one and all
Tell me to be the same, and walk tall

In the distant horizon, see the rising Sun
What does he say, the day has just begun

'Make the most as I throw my ray
Push your cares aside, and welcome the day'

The daffodils are dancing in the gentle breeze
The wildflowers are smiling with consummate ease

They all ask us to rejoice in the beautiful day
And raise our hearts, not losing the way

As I take my Barnie on his morning's walk
See a grey squirrel busy at his work

Chewing a little nut, sitting on his bushy tail
Asks us to be happy, and enjoy the day well

Suddenly become alive, the trees in the woods
They all are in such a jovial mood

Urge us to savour freely the sunny day
And say a prayer for the rain to stay away

Presently I hear the churchbell rings
Blessing from heaven, it most certainly brings

With gratitude in our hearts we all pray
And thank God for giving such a glorious day

JUST REMEMBER ME

Dispiriting yet sublime

Why is it so very hard to attend a funeral
Service, which doubtless is remarkably poignant
Why is it so heart-rending to say a farewell final
To a person in one's life was so significant

The vicar, in all earnest conducts the service
The attending crowd, big or small, watch with intent
Occasional cough, or blowing of the nose does no disservice
Everybody sings the hymns to his heart's content

A commentary of one's life, with ease and suffering is given
Certain things are revealed, which we wouln't have known
About achievement, high and low, of the deceased is spoken
Grateful thanks are offered, and merited respect shown

As the service ends, the coffin is escorted out
Some perhaps would say their very last farewell
Others would follow to the ultimate committal no doubt
And to the departing one, wish the journey well

Attending a funeral, especially of a dear friend
Is always hard, no matter what other people say
Dispiriting yet sublime it is, as the service ends
Thank God for giving us forbearance as we pray!

Hymie's 90th Birthday

They say when you have reached ten and three scores
Every day above that truly is a bonus
Now that you have attained one score more
Thank God being to you so very gracious

Nostalgia, no doubt will take you back
To those years, you have so gallantly journeyed
Through good and bad times, and success and setback
An enviable milestone, you have now achieved

You have been fortunate, round you to have a devoted family
And a circle of loyal friends, counting myself as one
I have admired your boundless energy unceasingly
And sincerity of purpose, doubt there was none

As we raise our glasses for your 90th. birthday
Pray God gives you good health and fortune
We wish you the very best for today and everyday
Long may you live, and be showered with His boon.

JUST REMEMBER ME

The Kittiwakes of Dunbar

Those beautiful Kittiwakes on the seafront of Dunbar
Most of them resting, a few on their short flights
On the rugged hills of the sunlit harbour
In their hundreds, what a wonderful sight

The continuous noise they make is so very shrill
'Kitti- wake'they sing non-stop to their hearts content
I listen and admire, they give me such a thrill
Oh, how I like to watch their every single movement

There I see the two of them, so very warm and loving
Wonder if they have just become mates, or are long-lovers
Sitting so close to one another, and busy caressing
Oblivious of the rest, in their own world for ever

Suddenly I see a little chick with his mother beside
Wonder if father is near, or gone to hunt a fish
The mother is making sure he stays by her side
And not stray, no doubt that would be his wish

Then there is the plump old man, sitting unusually quiet
Seemingly accepting the noise, and all goings on round
Appears not to be disgruntled, neither concerned about his weight
May be waiting for his call, yet his feet firm on the ground

Don't know how late they'll go on, perhaps as fades the light
Deserving their well earned rest, especially from the onlookers
Begin again in all earnest, when ends the night
Bringing life to the shores of the beautiful harbour

I walked round leisurely, it appeared to be for hours
Watched the Kittiwakes' movements, and heard them blissfully sing
Their non-stop singing still rings in my eager ears
How can I forget that beautiful sunny day of spring?

Attachment

Why is it we like someone
Why love someone else's touch
Why exception there is none
Why attachment we seek so much

With every bonding there is pain
We know it so very well
Yet in love fall time and again
Cannot resist its magic spell

So much suffering, so much hurt
A lesson, don't seem to learn
Whether near or far apart
Cannot fight our strong yearn

Not all however is doom and gloom
Of good times, there are lots
Sad ones of course have no room
Only happiness stays in our thoughts

Asked if one likes to be attached
And have the two, joy and pain
Or remain completely detached
Neither facing loss nor gain

I know what would be the answer
Can one justly remain detached
Neither rejoice, nor truly suffer
Ignoring the effect, we become attached

Three streakers

It was at a Test Cricket match at Old Trafford in Manchester
We saw three male Streakers, and not just one
The afternoon was sunny and hot, in early summer
Brightened up the day, the dullness of the play soon gone

A Psychiatrist myself, and a Judge-friend of mine
Were having a drink in the bar, with his wife, a Social worker
Their student teenage daughter was there, it was glorious sunshine
With the rest of the crowd we watched,, who greeted them with cheers

The first one came running from the ground's one end to another
The stewards just watched, did not do any chasing
We thought we had seen enough, more surprise followed sooner
When the second one came, all excited and flaunting

This time the stewards chased, he fell climbing over one barrier
Unceremoniously they led him out of our sight
Had we seen enough, beyond all our expectation followed another
Hugging one player, and trying on another, just imagine his plight

Couldn't help wondering, what must the streakers think
Were they so insensitive, gloating over their performance
Or were they fully aware, but something made them sink
And they became exhibitionists, losing their forbearance

Peering through his glasses the Judge said that he would send them all to prison
Said I jokingly, "What is wrong with free expression?"
His wife commentated, the betting money has swayed all rhyme and reason
The daughter kept quietly grinning, seemingly enjoying the occasion

JUST REMEMBER ME

As I drove home, asked myself, what makes a person bare all
In front of a big crowed, was it solely the booze
The day was very hot, was it the betting money after all
Or a defiance to the Establishment, wasn't there so much to lose?

The more I analysed, the more I concluded the reason for their action
We had counted four, wondered anything if I had missed
They did bring a light relief, judging by the crowd's reaction
If I were the Judge, I would have their cases summarily dismissed!

Charity

One afternoon I saw this pretty woman
Standing in a queue in the village Co-op
In my hand, I had two packs of Belgian buns
She kept on looking at them non-stop

Quizzically said I, 'Have you tried them?'
'No', she responded with a broad smile
'They are delicious, befitting the name'
'Would rather not', said in her inimitable style

Our conversation, then on were wide-ranging
The queue in front was very long
Discussed the horrible weather we were having
Her views on its effect were very strong

We were lucky in this part of Cheshire
Others in the Country were obviously not
Hull, Sheffield, Doncaster in East Yorkshire
Were still suffering, and counting the cost

She emphasised 'We send help to the World
What about our own people, when in need?
Why help so little, so late, and so hard?'
With her stern view, I completely agreed

They say, 'Charity begins at home'
Disaster of such a scale, makes one appreciate
Passing aid to the World, is it welcome
When sufferers here receive so little and so late

Lonely and alone

On a dark sombre night, lonely and alone
Reclining on a bedroom chair, I do ponder
In this vast world, there's nothing that I own
What good is life's journey, can't but wonder

Feel so downhearted, shoulders heavy and sunk
Is it not time that I say farewell to this world
All the bygone years appears completely blank
What good to carry on, totally uncared and unloved

Do I hear a sound, see a light flicker
Sit so still with ears and eyes open
Am pleasantly surprised to hear your whisper
And to feel your touch, a blessing from heaven

'You are not alone, will never be lonely'
Your gentle voice hear so very clear
'I am with you , and always will be'
The darkness lifts, the world again becomes dear!

JUST REMEMBER ME

Your whisper

In the deep of the night, lying half--awake
Could hear your voice, it was in a whisper
I knew for certain that was not a fake
Only what you were saying was not very clear

Having looked around, went to the front door
As I opened, could hear the patter of rain
Looked for you everywhere, scoured evermore
Oh, how I wished it was not in vain

Shut the front door, and looked inside everywhere
What wouldn't I give to hear what you said
My search was to no avail, found you nowhere
Went to bed in desperation, and there I stayed

Kept blaming myself for not hearing you clear
Why wasn't I fully awake, at least for once
Found fault with the rain of course for its pitter-patter
Wished you hadn't whispered, nor spoken from a distance

Kept tossing and turning, not able to sleep anymore
Waited in expectation in case you spoke again
This time would stay wide-awake for sure
Prayed that you speak once more, and ease my pain.

Your call

Who is calling me in the still of the night
Do I hear it wrong or am I hearing right

Am I thoroughly mistaken, or is it a genuine call
Or am I just dreaming, there is no voice at all

Is it truly you my dear, is it your voice
Or is it a big deception, over which have no choice

Whether real or otherwise, can sleep no more
Lie fully awake, my ears turned to the door

Oh, how I wish my love, it was sincerely you
Calling me by my name as sweet lovers do.

So in love

Why are you so in love
Why with him
Why in your mind's cove
Why in your dream

Why is he never apart
Why everywhere
Why is he in your heart
Why always there

Why has he such a spell
Why upon you
Why is it you can't tell
Why lovers do ?

I too was in love
I was once
Would rather nothing have
It was chance

I still see her face
Her love so esteem
Nothing could that efface
It was a dream

I was in love so
Was made in heaven
Lost her so long ago
But 'love' will never be forgotten!

A distant display of lights

Looking through the window, sitting in our 'plane
What a wonderful spectacle, a show of bright lights
As we approach Cologne, so very hard to refrain
From expressing our joy, in the dark of the night

Intermittently we have been looking through our window
As darkness fell, hardly anything to be seen
Suddenly before our eyes, was this wonderful show
Oh, to behold, how thrilled we have been

For miles and miles, we could see the lights glistening
At first it was from a distance, gradually came near
We knew very well, our destination was fast approaching
Soon the 'plane will touch down, and we would be there

The distant display of lights from the earth below
For once it was not up from the sky
How our eyes sparkled, to see the lights glow
Fondly I will remember till the day I die!

Germany,
26.8.07.

Full -Moon and I

Kölner Dom, I was passing by
There was Full-Moon in the sky
Standing of course on his own
I was also all alone

The city was there full of light
Did not need his this night
But I wanted him to be my own
Was so glad that he had shone

On holiday, I was in Germany
Was he also visiting, just like me
Or his duty, he was carrying on
Lighting the World, as he has always done

Heard his voice, loud and clear
'With you I am, have no fear'
Loneliness of mine had soon gone
No longer was I, lost and forlorn

Wondered how many were like me
Longing for a real company
Thanked God that his heart I had won
Happy at last, I moved on.

Germany,
27.8.07

JUST REMEMBER ME

Full Moon's company

We were journeying from Düsseldorf to Cologne
It was such a pleasant and peaceful night
The Full Moon in the sky standing on his own
Kept company all the way, to our delight

The train inside was full, it was a double-decker
We managed to find two seats, to our relief
As I looked up to the sky, there was no star
But the Moon in his fullness shining beyond belief

Wondered how long before we'll stop seeing the Full Moon
Kept looking intermittently through the train's window
Much to our pleasant surprise, that didn't happen soon
Stayed on till the journey's end, and delighted us so

We felt so safe that with us he journeyed
And secure that he kept his eyes on us all in the train
Was there a tinge of sadness, as our destination we reached
Thanked him from the bottom of our hearts, and hoped to see him again,

Germany,
30.8.07.

No poverty, no wealth

'Give us neither poverty, nor wealth'
Thus read the poster, outside Friends Meeting House
Was it a plea to have just enough by stealth
Or was its aim, more passion to rouse ?

Without poverty, we can certainly do
It matters not, weather of mind or material
Not having wealth, how can it be true
As we think of our very survival

All things considered, we must have wealth
The more the merrier, some would say
Poverty in the open, or coming by stealth
Nobody would disagree, can stay away

Asking for no wealth, neither poverty
Can one understand the reason behind
Is it hoped in all sincerity
Having neither will bring peace to the mind?

A little fox-cub

Silently I was walking through the woods
Mostly Silver Birches, with occasional Pine
Don't know why, but thought I should
On a Winter's day, the weather was fine

Rustling of the fallen leaves, and gentle wind
Did not seem to cause any stir
Nonchalantly I walked, there was nothing on my mind
Slowly but surely, breathing fresh air

Presently came across this thick bush
Was there a movement, was not very clear
I tiptoed along, there was a big hush
What did I see, was so very dear

A little fox-cub in deep sleep
Not a care on the earth, I could tell
Not wanting to wake him, a distance did keep
The thought of watching, I did dispel

Curled up snugly, such a beautiful creature
The nature had given him, his little den
Wondered where his parents gone, hoped not too far
Oblivious of any harm, was in his safe heaven

Walking quieter still, I left the scene
Prayed that he does not face any danger
No doubt his parents would bring food for him
He will wake up happier than ever!

New Year 2008

The New Year 2008 has just come
Barnie, my son and I give it a warm welcome

Hope it brings us health, happiness and peace
And the miseries of the world, it does ease

On our regular morning walk, we go next
Try to control Barnie's lead the very best

On a cold but dry morning, his pull I feel
With his boundless energy, he can't stay still

We see the big bare trees standing in the woods
The birds and the animals are in a happy mood

We wish them all a very happy New Year
They do reciprocate, we hear them cheer

After the morning's walk, we return home
Once again, we three give the New Year a hearty welcome!

Footprints on the Snow

Footprints on the Snow are so very dear
So distinct today, tomorrow they will disappear

Of all shapes and sizes, of birds, beasts, and humans
What a picturesque drawing on a glistening white canvas

Life is short, they make it starkly clear
Glory today, soon will no more be there

But memories will keep, the prints of the day
Try the hardest, nobody can take that away

At last there is something, for one to hold on
Not all is lost, not everything in life is gone!

Farewell to Harry

To our friend Harry, so very dear
Say, 'It has been so nice knowing you'
Now that you are going to a land so far
We all wish you the best, we really do

You were the very first Poet Laureate of Cheshire
We were privileged to have you ably conduct
The Poems and Pints' evenings with a confident air
In Congleton's Bear Town Tap with knowledge and tact

Oh, how I remember your generous welcome
Climbing up the steps, as I entered the Conference room
You made me feel completely at home
I was fortunate to become one of your flock soon

Over the past two years, that you I have known
Two poems you had recited, struck me most
One was about 'Food', with frantic gesticulation
The other following your divorce, you were so lost

Now that you're set to go to a distant land
Once again we wish our very best
Do spare a thought for these evenings in your home land
May be you'll become the first Poet Laureate of your new State!

JUST REMEMBER ME

The Tajmahal

There was the incomparable Taj, standing serene
Visited with a friend of mine, years ago
Today still stands, just as pristine
Memories took me back, endearingly so

Looking back to that day, I always remember
It was for two youths, wonder and reverence
That very first visit, forget I will never
The sun beaming upon, a singular experience

One can use adjectives, as many one wants
Nothing could do justice to that visit
They all fall short, explain they can't
That intense feeling, to see the Taj sunlit

We spent a full day, looking every nook and corner
Wandered in the grounds, and after went inside
It was so peaceful couldn't but wonder
At the 'Marvel in marbles', looking from outside

As we said 'goodbye', I made a promise
Next time I come, it will be with my wife
Years after, my dream, I did realise
Visited the Taj together, an inimitable experience in life

This time we saw the Monument by moonlight
Fortunately for us, the Full Moon was there
The glistening marbles, in the still of the night
Holding hands we walked, it was peace everywhere

With a pain deep in the heart, a sigh, and a tear
An Emperor's love of his wife, made truly eternal
The Taj by moonlight, the most revered star
We were simply overwhelmed, visiting the unique memorial!

JUST REMEMBER ME

My love

No matter how strong, I hold your hand
One thing I know, is for certain
There will come a day, when I leave this land
I may not wish, but have to loosen

Our first meeting, and all since happened
Our wedding; the birth of our son
Our lives together, joyful and saddened
Will last evermore, nothing would be gone

Memories will be there, stronger than ever
There will be a time, no doubt will fade
Holding our hands, so in love together
Will remain alive, not be put in shade

It was destiny, that we first met
Together we journeyed, it had to be so
Of course there were both joy and regret
With ups and downs, and stop and go

When the day comes, and I do loosen
The firm grip of my steady hand
"Meeting and Parting" there but to happen
My love will endure, know that you'll understand.

Puppies in the Kennel

The puppies in the Kennel are so sweet
Of different breeds, they are a treat

Of all shapes and sizes, in their own cubicles
Of varied colours, what a spectacle

On his own, or as I count five
Are so cute, so hard to describe

Most are busy at something, some are not
Lying huddled together, in sleep a lot

There I see one asleep in his food-bowl
Another one is busy playing a little ball

In the saw-dust, two are sleeping huddled in a corner
Five others are playing merrily with one another

One lot I see, standing up near the glass-front
Is it to say 'Hello', or to come out they want?

One is drinking water, another biting his empty bowl
In their activity, there is always a goal

In their own world, they are all happy
I look very hard, not one is unhappy

I wondered if at all they know about their fate
Where will they end up, sooner or late

There again us humans, foresee we cannot
Whether babies or grown-ups, just accept our lots

I remember well, how was it with Barnie
Two Airedale puppies, playing so joyfully

As we watched to us, one came over
That magic moment, forget I will never

We were in our worlds, to each other unknown
Two unknown worlds, became 'one' known

How destiny played truly its part
How sweet Barnie won over our hearts!

Unfair treatment

Two little children, a boy and a girl
Managed to climb up this low wall

Of the 'Side Portal' in front of Dom of Cologne
Did not think they were on their own

Soon came along the parents, a fairly young couple
Father got the girl down, after a little struggle

Mother kept taking photographs of the little boy
In all sorts of poses, he was like a toy

The girl wanted her share, but father wouldn't let
She had a little cry, that's as far she could get

The boy was then helped to climb down
They all left the scene, and headed for the town

Sitting on a bench, away not too far
I thought the parents were totally unfair

The girl did not get her fair share
What a disadvantage in upbringing, she has to bear

Wondered if that is how, starts a girl's life
Not a plain sailing, it is always a strife!

Germany,
19.8.08

A left-behind item

Seated on a stone-seat, in front of an Advert-stand
On a sunny afternoon, outside Kaufhof in Cologne
Saw cone rushing, this woman with bags in her hand
She stooped to pick up a shopping bag, resting on its own

Could feel her sense of relief, as up the bag she picked
Don't know why she thanked me, sincerely from her heart
Her inadvertent mistake, in leaving one bag, she must have realised
Was immensely pleased to find it untouched and intact

Why thank me at all, could not help but wonder
Did she think the bag, I really was guarding
That she was totally mistaken, I dared not tell her
I had not even noticed, that beside me it was resting

She left in a hurry, as fast she came
Don't know why I really was pleased at her gain
At least she recouped her left-behind item
I even got a 'vielen danke', in the bargain!

Germany,
19.8.08.

An unexpected encounter

After a nice cup of coffee, I kept walking along
On the side of a busy road, saw this little thing
A tiny little dead mouse; wondered how long
Also how did he meet his end, so peacefully lying

It was after our usual morning visit to Cafe Sagui
Beside the Espirit shop in the little square
On our holiday in Cologne, my son and I
Having enjoyed our Cappuccino in a nice atmosphere

My son went shopping, heading for the Hohe Strasse
Don't know why I strolled along to the book shop in the corner
Looking back, how I wished, had not proceeded that way
Was there a hand of fate, the dead mouse to encounter

Lying completely motionless, was this tiny little creature
The world passing by, everybody in a hurry
So peacefully he lay, death not able to alter
His graceful countanance, with no more worries

I paused for a moment, and said a little prayer
God only knows when his body will be moved
Such a tiny thing, his life made even shorter
Thanked God for our encounter, even though do little I could!

Germany,
23.8.08.

Love is lovelier second time round

Love is lovelier second time round
Why did I fall in love with you
I was still so honour-bound
With the lovely girl, I was wedded to

Why did I fall for your charms
Was it me or us to blame
Why did I hold you in my arms
Will our lives ever be the same?

Does one think in all conscience
I certainly did not, as in love I fell
Do lovers ever wonder of the consequence
As they come under one another's spell

Now I know that love is truly blind
As I hold you near my heart
There is only one thing on a lover's mind
All ideations are torn apart

All sorts of reasons, one tends to offer
Are they not excuses, can they justly explain
'Something new', aren't we always after
Blaming the 'old' over and again!

JUST REMEMBER ME

After Forty years

It was after a gap of almost Forty years
The two lovers once again did meet
There was no joy, neither shedding of tears
Their faces however were so lit

The meeting happened outside a Pub in Shropshire
On a bitterly cold December day
Slippery icy groundfrost was everywhere
Dull and dreary, the sky was grey

Walking carefully they approached one another
They had come early, the Pub wasn't yet open
Decided to walk back to sit in his car
Not even a kiss, had they really forgotten

Was it an after-thought, he gave her a kiss
Just a peck, she held her lips closed
Wouldn't have been better to give it a miss
The flames of yester year, were they so cold

Was there a fore-planning, either had made
Seemed to evaporate soon in thin air
Or was it because they were older and aged
Controlling wilfully any indiscreet ardour

Sitting in the car, old and recent times recalling
So much to catch up, about so much to talk
Holding hands cast aside, only occasional tapping
Both long retired, little discussion about work

Time just flew, the Pub was now open
Walking carefully together, they went inside
Because of the weather, not many places were taken
Ambience was warm, with Christmas decorations beside

They selected a table, sat facing one another
The waitress came, and greeted them with care

JUST REMEMBER ME

They selected a Christmas meal, the first time on offer
The service was superb, the food couldn't have been tastier

The conversation continued in between eating
It was non-stop, so much ground to cover
Occasional 'slip up' of the old time romancing
And exchange of glances, alluring as ever

At the end of the lunch, he went to settle the bill
Suddenly she was in a hurry, and ready to leave
This time not even a peck, what a big deal
He wondered if the re-union was genuine or make-believe

Forty years is a long time, so many things had happened
There had been gains and losses, both joy and despair
Forty years older now, have events truly dampened
Any hope of re-bonding of the lovers of yester year?

New Year 2009

2009, the New Year has come
Let us give it a hearty welcome

To 2008, we say a fond farewell
On the whole it was sensibly well

Goodbye to the old, and welcome to the new
It is a rule, avoid we can't do

Let us be grateful what 2008 had brought
Good, bad, or indifferent, we wanted or not

We genuinely hope, 2009 is better
In everyway, each day of the year

On our morning's walk, Barnie and me
Wish a happy New Year to everyone we., see

I can hear, they do reciprocate
With a big smile, they wish us the best

Barnie, my son, and me, the three of us together
Give 2009 again a welcome warm and sincere.

A phone call

The telephone rang, on a peaceful evening
Could hear my son duly answering

Had taken my Barnie for his walk
Just about managed to come back

Promptly he took over Barnie's lead
To answer the phone, I did proceed

The call was from my sister-in-law's son
To break the news of her passing on

To me, it came as a brutal shock
I was totally and utterly dumbstruck

Somehow recovering, after a few moments
Asked him to recount the sequence of events

That he was distraught, I could tell
Still managed to describe them well

I told him that he would find strength from God
Prayed for her soul's peace, looking up to the Lord

Realized sadly, how a simple call on phone
Unsettles one forever, with life's tranquillity gone!

Our Resi

Each year when on our holiday in Cologne
We would visit Resi, my sister-in-law
My son would accompany, I won't be alone
To see us both, how her eyes would glow

The welcome she gave, was truly from her heart
We used to visit her on a Sunday
When the time came for us to part
How we all wished, on we could stay

She was so warm, and such a kind hostess
We felt at home, each time we were with her
The six red roses we brought, she would so caress
Place them in her favourite vase, for all to admire

She would make us a nice meal, all home-made
There was of course for us, plenty to drink
She would make sure that we were well fed
Her meticulous attention was more than one'd think

So many photographs of our visit, we would take
Inevitably she would pose with myself or my son
Giving a generous smile, not just for the camera's sake
Oh, What a joyful reminder were they of our vacation

We used to invite her to come to town
Her favourite restaurant was Cafe Reichard
It would be for us all an enjoyable afternoon
Relishing their food, and looking at the Dom courtyard

Last few years, could see a surreptitious change
She began to complain regularly about her heart
No more preparing food of a wide range
Welcome though genuine, that ceased to be a part

She would also turn our sincere invitation down
To join us on an afternoon in Cafe Reichard

JUST REMEMBER ME

I was slow to appreciate her reluctance to come to town
Her failing health obviously payde a big part

She also had the hassle of changing apartment
From where she lived for years, to one much smaller
It must have been for her a big disappointment
The physical strain on top, did not help either

Last holiday, we saw her in her new apartment
She entertained us with shop-purchased cakes and coffee
We congratulated her for her organization and adjustment
Prayed to God in her new place, she will be happy

Last time I spoke to her, was on telephone
Wished her a merry Christmas, and ah happy birthday
I sensed quite a lot of anxiety in her tone
Asked me if we were coming to Kölner carnival on holiday

I thought for her to make that request was most unusual
Also in her conversation, sensed some confusion
On reflection, now realize, the happening was gradual
Perhaps she had not been regular also with her medication

Within a couple of weeks, we received a telephone call
Her son rang to give us the worst news
"God will give you strength", I said, as do recall
"The blessing of your mother will always be with you"

We both attended her funeral, my son and I
As the coffin was laid to rest, said a fond farewell
The six red roses we brought, gently threw them with a sigh
She will caress them as ever, I know it well!

JUST REMEMBER ME

An unwelcome Prince

That heavy front door in our hall
Undoubtedly is the most frequented one
Young, old, fat, thin, also short and tall
Everybody comes and goes, till the day is done

Barnie is no exception, our pet dog
One thing is noticeable, there aren't many pets
Who come and go through, for me to log
As to any unwanted visitor, hasn't happened yet

One day however, most unexpected, what did I see
To take Barnie out, as I opened the door
This 'princely' little frog waiting so patiently
Wanting to come in, squatting on the porch floor

Before I could close the heavy door, he leapt inside
In a flash, I was totally dumbfounded
Barnie kept barking loud, standing outside
With his lead in my hand, I was overstretched

He might look 'princely', but was not welcome
An unwanted visitor, I had to get him out
Was he in need of warmth, or a welcoming home
Most certainly, that wasn't the way to go about

It wasn't much of a struggle, before I managed to catch
Unkindly put him out, with a somewhat mixed feeling
At least I had saved him from Barnie's vicious clutch
Hoped he found a niche, in the nature, ever welcoming!

The little Robin

Each, time I mow our lawns, see this pretty little Robin
Comes so near, and perches sweetly on the wheelbarrow
After all this time, I feel that I truly know him
He knows me too, oh, how he lets me know

I see his red breast, and hear him twitter
Sitting on the half-filled barrow, with freshly cut grass
Wonder if it's me, or the fresh cutting he is after
In case he finds a worm, not appearing to be crass

He urges me to come out, and mow the lawns more often
So that he can come, and keep me company
I must not let the grass grow too high and sloven
He will also look for food, in case there's any

There I see him fly away, as fast he came
Returned in no time, what for I wonder
Why can't he sit still, is he playing a game
Making sure I notice him, distracting from the lawn-mower

As I nearly finish mowing, see him fly away
Hope he found some food, upon trying his best
We both know well that we will meet another day
When I will mow the lawns, and he would be my prize guest

April Fool

Twenty years ago, that day of April
Oh, how I remember, and always will

Every single moment of that fateful day
Is so alive, and will remain that way

Woke up in the morning, the sun shone bright
Opening the window curtains, let in the light

Helped my dear wife get out of bed,
Last few days not well, needed some aid

She began doing household chores, cooked her breakfast
I thought the corner for us had turned at last

She even used the washing machine, later watched telly
I spent the afternoon, mowing the lawns busily

In the night, she retired early to bed
Asked me to join, also rest my head

At one point I mentioned, the day was first of April
Not once she had fooled me, was that her will

I remember well, that my query she did not answer
Was it deliberate, or an omission most unlike her

Clasping my hand firm, thanked me for all I had done
I said, 'Not me, thank God that our worries are bygone'

Meeting and parting are but life's golden rule
Near midnight, dying in my arms, she made me the biggest April Fool!

Written on the occasion of the twentieth Anniversary of my wife's passing away.

The beautiful pheasant

The beautiful pheasant, resting on the table
Is he just sleeping, or really dead
Is he not trying, or simply not able
As he would like, to raise his body and head

Lying completely motionless, and still warm
His multicoloured body is truly captivating
Oh, how I wish to lift him in my arms
To see him in that state, is so heart-rending

Could picture it was only hours ago
He was freely roaming a busy country road
A brutal knock ended his young life so
Did he deserve this, I ask the Lord

Enquire as much I like, get no answer
I know fully well, there is not any
Explanations, and blames, are plenty on offer
To me, loss of a life is one too many

Did not like to ask, what would be his fate
He is already dead, does it at all matter
Wonder if his girl is still waiting for her mate
One thing is certain, will have to count on for ever!

2.4.09.

That Magnolia tree

That beautiful Magnolia tree in our back garden
To see in full bloom, as comes the Spring
The nature all round, oh, how it does brighten
Each time I look, what a joy it brings

I remember well when the buds began to appear
In expectation watched, as they opened more each day
The tree at last in full bloom with flowers all over
Outshining all the rest, stands so grand in every way

As I look at the tree in its full bloom
Any time of the day, or even at night
Takes away life's all the doom and gloom
Everything I gaze upon appears so very bright

I know only too well, it will not long last
The flowers would disappear, leaving the tree on its own
Other trees no doubt will try to play their part
Will life be the same, once the sweet flowers are gone

Spring will come again, the tree will be in full bloom
Outshining the rest once more, will bring delight
Once again it will take away all the earth's gloom
Wonder if I will be there to share the amazing sight!

JUST REMEMBER ME

The crimson coloured Rhododendron

Of all the Rhododendron trees in our garden
That crimson coloured one, I like best
As it begins to bloom, I feel I am in heaven
To see it in full glory, I can hardly wait

Each day I see the flowers open up a bit more
Those gorgeous crimsons brighten up the nature
As they begin to blossom, I so adore
Interspersed with green leaves, become the garden's feature

Looking round the garden, all I see is green
The crimson flowers are the first to open
With their wonderful sparkle, are so pristine
Is anything more refreshing, I ask so often

Other Rhodos start to appear, one after another
But not one can ever take the crimson's place
Outshining the rest, with its unique feature
Brightens up my world, with its amazing grace

I know very well, one day the flowers would be gone
Leaving the tree on its own, but for the green leaves
Wonder like me, if the tree will also mourn
The passing of the crimson flowers, with moist eyes.

JUST REMEMBER ME

The unveiling ceremony of R.S.M.'s Wall of Honour

The year was 2009, 12th of July the date
The venue was R.S.M. in London, the purpose to celebrate

The unveiling of its newly erected Wall of Honour
My son and I were amongst its biggest gathering ever

The members could bring guests for the occasion
My son came along with me to the celebration

The occasion though sombre, the atmosphere was festive
Everybody we saw, appeared so agile and active

A gathering of all Nationalities, age and sex no bar
It was so nice to see babies in arms, and of course toddlers

The whole R.S.M. family had gathered to celebrate
A most venerable event, and show their respect

The President addressed the audience in the main Lecture Hall
The Society's past, present, and future, explaining them all

After a drinks reception, the audience gathered for the unveiling
The Atrium was full to the brim so was the corridors surrounding

We managed to get prime positions, my son made that sure
All through the ceremony, with him beside, I felt secure

Three poets recited poems, one by the past Poet Laureate
They were befitting the occasion, everybody did appreciate

The two Vice-Presidents and the President, one after the other
Read out the names of those who were receiving the honour

JUST REMEMBER ME

My son alerted me, soon my name will be read
Pleased though I was, felt truly humbled

At last came the time, we all have been waiting for
The removal of curtains from the Wall of Honour

There were nine of them, taken off one by one
Gracefully they were removed, left behind was none

They all clapped their hands, as each curtain was removed
To see the inscribed names on the glass wall, everybody was moved

No function would be complete without provision of refreshment after
Food and drinks were plentiful, and best services on offer

In between the refreshments, people kept circulating
There was a sense of achievement, a sensible merry-making

The President circulated well, speaking to groups or individuals
I managed a few words, thanked him for his speech and the Wall

They took photographs of the Wall and of each other
No doubt for a nostalgic look, may be years after

We were so pleased to meet Patil, the Development Director, and his family
Complimented him for his hard work, and thanked him profusely

As we left the R.S.M. building, we had a sense of achievement
It was a momentous day, and enjoyed its every moment!

A chatterbox

After attending a celebration in R.S.M. in London
I was on a train journey to Crewe from Euston

Ahead of me was Sunday's three hours trip
Was so looking forward to a well earned kip

Slowly but surely became full our compartment
The two empty seats facing me soon had their occupant

A couple in their sixties, may be somewhat older
Perched on them with the greatest ease and pleasure

Hardly he was seated, the husband began talking to me
And carried on relentless all through the journey

He made it soon obvious, by profession he was a lawyer
After some persuasion, I told him I was a Medical doctor

We discussed all topics possible under the sun
Not just relating to serious issues, but also to fun

I was pleasantly surprised that on most issues we agreed
The social structure declining with drugs, crime, and greed

I felt sorry for his wife, who sat through it all silent
As her husband carried on totally unrepentant

There was only one brief pause when he went to visit the toilets
She hoped sincerely that I didn't mind his garrulous outlets

Before she went further, I said I knew the feeling
To put up with a chatterbox husband must be heart-rending

He resumed his chattering vigorously hardly he returned to his seat
In a voice, mostly loud, displaying no discreet

JUST REMEMBER ME

Occasionally he would bend over, and speak in a low voice
To underline a point, leaving me hardly any choice

At last I reached Crewe station, was there a sigh of relief
A chatterbox will never change, became my unswerving belief.

Completed in Germany,
14.8.09.

JUST REMEMBER ME

My Seventieth Birthday

I have reached three scores and ten
From now on every day is a bonus
For this I can only thank heaven
I look up, and duly say my prayers

I look back as someone said rightly
'The future does not belong to any one
So we look to the past', not merely
To re-live some happenings of days gone

It is then, things have actually happened
No pretence, neither imagination, but real
May be good, bad, may be indifferent
It is there, one certainly can tell

I have had many ups and downs
Seen successes, faced share of failures
Fulfilled wishes, still many unfulfilled ones
Is not that the life's usual course ?

Was lucky to reach top of my profession
Listened to people, who came with their woes
Like to feel, made some contribution
Towards the relief of their many sorrows

Have been lucky to have a good family
Good neighbours, and a few good friends
All in all, life's been blessed really
Until the blow of my wife's demise

Two events in all my Seventy years
Will remain uppermost, rest of my life
One with joy, the other with tears
Our son's birth, the death of my wife

Thankful to God, it was my son
Who helped me along in my need

JUST REMEMBER ME

Don't know what I would have done
When I lost my wife, truly indeed?

Only two wishes left for me now
Please God, He helps me fulfil
From our place, take my last bow
With a pretty girl, my son does settle

On this, my Seventieth Birthday
Wish the World the best one can wish
Peace on Earth to-day and every day
May the good will never diminish.

There is that of God

There is that of God in everyone
Whether one has faith or has none

Whether one is old, or one is young
Whether one is right or one is wrong

Whether one has wealth, or is very poor
Whether one is welcoming, or soon shows the door

Whether one is erudite or illiterate
Whether one is bright or in a vegetative state

Whether one is a crook, or honest as can be
Whether one is full of greed, or all generosity

Whether one is sinful, or very religious
Whether one is ordinary, or very famous

Whether one is miserable, or full of gaiety
Whether one is a slowcoach, or all alacrity

Whether one is a loner, or so gregarious
Whether one is a born-loser, or always victorious

Whether one is glamorous, or very ugly
Whether one is amorous, or so unfriendly

Whether one is inactive, or very busy
Whether one is nervous, or going easy

Whether one is mobile, or in a wheelchair
Whether one is careful, or does not care

Whether one is garrulous, or not so chirpy
Whether one lives in a cuckoo-land, or very earthly

Whether one is strong, or very weak
Whether one is aggressive, or so meek

Whether one is affable, or very haughty
Whether one is humble, or thinks he is God almighty

There is that of God in everyone
It is so evident when the day is done!

Gentleness and humility

'Only the gentle are ever really strong'
One doesn't need to look hard and long

They say, 'Knowledge makes one humble'
Likewise having strength one becomes gentle

The more you know, the more you realise
How little you know, that makes you humble and wise

You don't need to be hard, to show your strength
To prove you have it, don't need to go any length

The fact that you possess, makes you gentle
The more knowledge one has, makes him humble.

JUST REMEMBER ME

Our visit to Resi

It was on a beautiful sunny August afternoon
My son and I visited the cemetery in Sud Friedhof
To see our Resi resting, not any more on her own
With her husband beside, peacefully sure enough

We both attended her funeral, way back in January
That was on a snow-covered bitterly cold day
This time the sun was shining, brightly as can be
The gloom of that former trip, seemed to be far away

Arriving at the cemetery we began to look for the grave
On our last trip had a rough idea where it was
Our search was to no avail, at last up we gave
Went to the Caretaker, for him to properly direct us

A tall thin middleaged man, with two shaking hands
I gave him the details of our Resi's passing away
He scanned through his age-old system, no computer to hand
Gave me a proper direction, so that we didn't stray

We then strolled along to find the sought-after grave
My son spotted it, did not have to go too far
We were so pleased to see her name beautifully engraved
Underneath her husband's, in letters so very clear

The six red roses we brought, placed them between the two
Knew well she will share them with her beloved spouse
In the past when we brought, she would be so delighted too
And place them in her special vase in the lounge of her house

We stayed with them quite a while, and talked to our Resi
Reminded her of the times of our Sunday visits
When she would entertain us, and was truly busy
Preparing a most delicious meal, for us to savour and eat

On this first visit to her grave, we did not feel at all sad
Unlike the time of our last trip, in the bitterly cold winter
Knew to see us two together, she was so very glad
It was so nice to see Resi again, on our holiday in Summer!

Germany, 17.8.09.

Back to back

Sitting on a bench in the Seiten Portal
In front of Kölner Dom, in the corner
My eyes wander, as only usual
At the goings on, both near and far

Presently not far, what do I see
Sitting on a bench, an elderly couple
Looking for a back-rest, there isn't any
To rest their backs, find it a struggle

Soon they discover a clever way out
Sat with their backs confronting each other
It was a respite, there was no doubt
Even pretended to fall asleep, with no care

Sitting not too far, I see another world
The elderly couple still so in love
In between resting, they exchange loving words
Long may they live, I pray to the gods above.

Germany,
18.8.09.

Just remember me

On an August afternoon, in glorious stmshine
I went to sit on the bank of river.Rhine

In my favourite place next to the kiosk
Between Fähre Köln Messe and Hohenzollern brücke

As I approached the spot, looked for Fähre Köln Messe
Somehow the ferry boat appeared different in every way

This man I saw standing relaxed next to the kiosk
Asked him the boat's name, said it was 'Strolch'

For a moment felt upset, thought had lost my favourite boat
But his reassuring was strong, with a high note

I took photos as in the past, but with an uncertain mind
A lingering doubt was there, couldn't leave behind

Sitting in my favourite spot adjacent to the kiosk
Kept looking at the Rhine, the Messe, the trains and the brücke

In between I saw this man walking down the steps
Went to the boat, inside and out, adjusting bits and pieces

After a while, up he came, and presented me with two photos
They were of 'Strolch' thus ending my anxiety and woes

I asked him 'wie viel', he did not want any money
With a smile,   said in English,'Just remember me'

I said, of course I will, and then shook his hands
Having said, 'Auf wiedersehen', was left in a wonderland

As I left, don't know why, went close to look at the boat once more
This time I could see clear the name 'Strolch' as never before

Germany,
19.8.09.

God's blessing

As I kneel down, and say my prayer
Almighty God, I know you are there

Stooping down low, as I touch your feet
With such veneration, and joy so sweet

The touch of your hands on my bowed head
Oh, how it helps to forge ahead

Nothing is more sublime in this wide world
Than your blessing, to count on, my Lord

I hope it evermore with me stays
To show me the way, for now and always.

About the Author

Dr. G.C. Kanjilal is a retired Consulatant Psychiatrist, who has lived in the village of Cranage in Cheshire, for over 38 years.

His interest in poetry goes back to his childhood years when his interest in nature was influenced by Wordsworth's work.

In rural Cheshire, he has been able to develop his sentiments with an analytical look of his profession.

He lost his wife, Nana, in 1989, and now lives with his son, Arun and their latest pet Airedale, Barnie.

By the same author

By the same author

By the same author

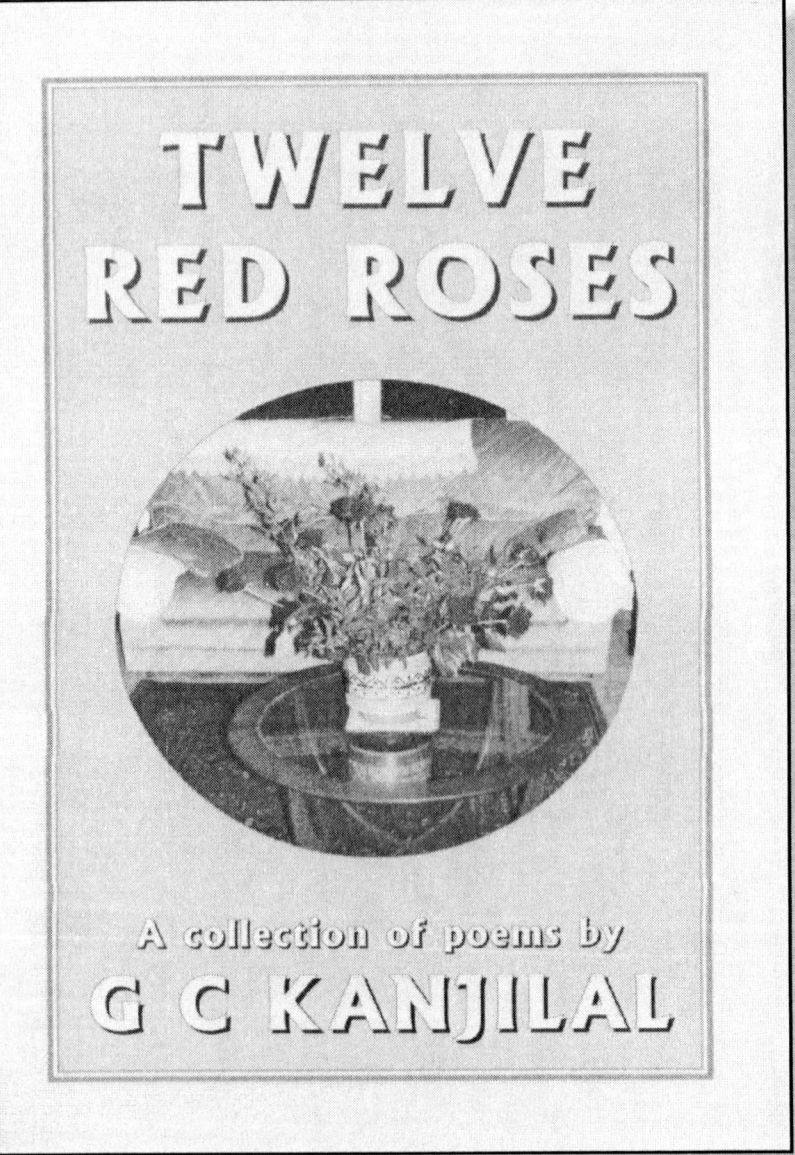